# A
# Nuneaton
# Childhood
## in the 1950s

# A Nuneaton Childhood
## in the 1950s

*To Trevor*
*All the best*

Peter Lee

*Jan 2016*

AMBERLEY

Bridge Street.

First published 2014

Amberley Publishing
The Hill, Stroud
Gloucestershire, GL5 4EP

www.amberley-books.com

Copyright © Peter Lee, 2014

The right of Peter Lee to be identified as the Author
of this work has been asserted in accordance with the
Copyrights, Designs and Patents Act 1988.

British Library Cataloguing in Publication Data.
A catalogue record for this book is available from the British Library.

ISBN 978 1 4456 4153 9 (print)

ISBN 978 1 4456 4167 6 (ebook)

Typesetting and Origination by Amberley Publishing.
Printed in Great Britain.

# Contents

# Introduction

This is not a very remarkable tale. I was born and brought up a working-class kid in an industrial town in the Midlands. The only difference is that I have taken the opportunity to write it down before I disappear into the ether and my life is almost completely forgotten. Although we were thoroughly working class (my dad was a big union man and life-long socialist), we were not poor in the conventional sense.

By the mid-1950s, there were four incomes coming into our household, both my dad and brother Jim by that time worked at Keresley Colliery. My mother was a seamstress at George Eliot Hospital and Granny Lee (who died in 1957) worked in the canteen at Courtaulds factory in Marlborough Road. Granny Lee and my mother always kept a good table, and worked very hard to keep everyone in the family and our family home clean and tidy. In fact, I can say without a shadow of doubt that I owe my fastidious habits in dress, cleanliness and decorum to my mother. She laboured against the odds to keep her family clean. We only had one cold tap, a copper in the kitchen, a cast-iron range and no inside toilet. In the morning, I set out to school in a very cleanly manner, although by the time I was finished for the day my appearance had deteriorated, like most little boys, into an advanced state of dishevelment.

The only unusual thing about me was that I grew to have an unusual empathy with the town in which I was born and grew up. This has led to me being called a 'local historian' today. I tend to rail against this term because it seems, in this 'jobsworth' age, that people try to class everybody as something. I, on the other hand, just see myself as someone interested in the place where I have lived for over sixty years. Another effect of my childhood conditioning was that I developed a lifelong passion for railways, and steam trains in particular. I skipped a period when first-generation diesels and electrics came in, which I hated with a vengeance. This may have coincided with taking an

Riversley Park boats. (*Courtesy Colin Yorke*)

Riversley Park café was popular in the 1950s. It was where we bought our pop and ice creams.

Few images illustrate the grim reality of old Nuneaton more than this view of Wheat Street before Vicarage Street ring road was built when Wheat Street led out to Oaston Road.

Another view of Bridge Street.

This view of St Nicholas' parish church has stood the test of time, surrounded by its ancient graveyard.

Queens Road.

Riversley Park in winter. (*Reg. Bull*)

increased interest in the opposite sex, to the exclusion of less heroic and manly activities. I happily enjoy super-slick electric train journeys today, only as a means of getting from A to B as fast as possible, because work has conditioned me to live in the fast lane (and these things are very fast indeed).

Although we were able to live life in an exemplary way as working-class people, I acknowledge today the role my parents played in facilitating this. They led good lives, working hard, caring for and being sensitive and considerate towards others. My mother, in particular, skivvied way beyond the immediate needs of the family. She always looked out for her friends' families as well, and she developed lifelong friendships through her outgoing personality, which I did not necessarily appreciate at the time (as you will see later). I can remember never having rows in the family, and us kids generally (but not always) behaved ourselves, not least because we did not want to upset our Mam. Not my dad, however, as in the disciplinary department our mother was the first arbiter of correction. I can hear her say now, 'Tell our Peter off, for what he's just done', and my dad saying words to the effect of, 'Look, you're getting yourself into trouble and with me for not having a quiet life.' Being kids, of course, meant that sometimes we did cross the boundary into naughtiness, or scruffiness, or forgetfulness, but we knew once our mother fixed us with that gimlet eye we were in trouble. So the boundaries were clearly defined early on and we knew to avoid the consequences as much as possible.

Like many older people today, I despair at the perceived general deterioration in standards in everyday life. In my opinion, so many people you see represented on the television, and in soap operas particularly, have extremely poor attitudes both to their own general conduct and to others. This must have a drip-feed effect on modern kids. I am thankful that I was brought up in an age of boundaries and knowing right from wrong, where kids did not grizzle and prattle loudly in public places, and were conscious of the feelings of others. The old days have gone I am afraid, but in my case are not entirely forgotten.

Peter Lee, Nuneaton

# Chapter One

# A Nuneaton Childhood

I read somewhere that childhood is all about excitement, and old age is about contentment. When I was a kid in Nuneaton in the 1950s there was not much excitement around and one had to be content with what little bits of fun you had. You kind of expanded on the boredom as best you could.

It was an age of austerity after the Second World War, and Nuneaton was then just getting over its wartime experiences. The old town was grim and dirty. We knew no better, of course, as there were no computers or internet, high-tech gadgetry of any description, and pop music was pretty basic stuff. There was no television either. My family did not get its first grainy black-and-white set until the mid-1950s, possibly as late as 1957, and I hardly recall what we watched in those days. *Andy Pandy*, *Bill & Ben*, and later *Emergency Ward 10* perhaps? Television was distinctly unmemorable. For me at any rate, there were no programmes I can think of that I particularly enjoyed, other than *Bill & Ben* because they talked so daftly!

One of my very early memories, of being wheeled along in my pram along Coton Road, is clear. I always remember that pram because it had a cool hood over it with a little fringe around the sides, and I recall in my mind's eye it being a warm, summery day. Looking down Coton Road towards the town centre, I sat up in the pram and peered through the tassels. This was the old Coton Road before it was made into a dual carriageway. Why I should remember that singular moment I have no idea. In later years, my mam said she would regularly take me into Riversley Park on a warm day for a nice walk and sit on a park bench. I guess the real reason was to see who was about, and have a chat to friends and passing acquaintances. My mam had an uncanny knack of striking up conversations with, what seemed to me, complete strangers. In some cases, this was much to my embarrassment. I showed a lack of patience because I got so thoroughly bored. There was only so much kicking pebbles

That pram.

Riversley Park in the 1950s. The flower displays then were as good as today (if not better). This was a popular meeting place for my mother to wheel my pram on a warm sunny day. Wasn't every day warm and sunny in the '50s? (*Geoff Edmands*)

and stamping on ants one could do within the orbit of my mother's attention without being told off.

We forget now, of course, that in the 1950s Nuneaton people knew each other far more intimately than we do now. We can go into town today and spend hours there without recognising anyone or striking up a conversation with strangers, other than a shop assistant. In order to get about you walked, and if you saw someone with whom you had a nodding acquaintance you always said 'Good Morning'. My parents could expand on this by progressing to 'looks like its going to rain this afternoon', and fifteen minutes to an hour later they would still be gossiping while I stood there fidgeting, losing the will to live, and finally mythering them to come on ('Mam, I'm bored'). I think my dad lost patience with Mam from time to time too, because there are only a certain number of houses to go around in a conversation, and my mam was good at padding it out.

This was how adults filled their leisure hours. 'Nattering' we called it. Let's face it – back then there was not much to talk about either, and I remember the conversation often steering towards old Mrs so-and-so's husband passing away. This would lead to discussion about other people they mutually knew, their ailments, families and personal (and supposedly private) goings on. This instilled in me a desire for a certain amount of privacy in my life. I didn't want Mrs so-and-so talking about me, and to be the focus of other people's gossip.

The Lee side of my family came from Leicester and, particularly when my old Granny Lee was alive (she died in 1957), a lot of weekends we travelled over to Leicester, to villages such as Glenfield and down the Narborough Road where our relations lived. I always recall these visits, because it usually either involved a nice train ride from Abbey Street station or a bumpy Midland Red bus trip (the No. 658, as I recall). When we reached Leicester, we changed to another local bus that trundled us out to the relatives. I still have affection for these old methods of transport, grim and slow though they were. After an hour sitting on one of the old Midland Red hard mocquette seats with chromed metalwork, listening to the distinctive growl of the engine, my fidgety bum went numb.

I have a great deal of affection too for my old family in Leicester. They were an interesting lot, to me at any rate. We never had any known Lee relatives out there, because we had lost touch with them many years before because my Granddad Lee had died from pneumonia in 1927. Granny Lee was originally a Davis, and I remember she had several sisters: Auntie Maggie, Auntie Jessie and Auntie Ethel. There were other siblings who died before I was conscious of the

James Walter Lee, (1883–1927). My Grandfather, photographed here as a boy, died very young from pneumonia contracted after he had an accident on a bike.

My mum, me as a baby, our Jim and his rabbit in 1948. Jim bred rabbits for years before turning to budgies and our mongrel dog called Chummy. This is the back garden of our house in Norman Avenue and the backs of houses we can see here are in Edward Street. The old gentleman who lived directly over the fence in the background (Mr Thorpe) lost his arm in the First World War. He's dead now, of course, but I can always remember him, a lovely old chap with a white stocking over his stump. It worried me as a kid seeing his arm like that – it just did not seem right, and I did not know why it was like that, for the horrors of the trenches had not been explained to me. Our old dog Chummy had a girlfriend, a sausage dog, who trotted up our entry and barked at the gate for Chummy to come out to play. I can see them now, pottering together down the street nuzzling each other. There was nothing in it, they were just good friends. There were so few cars around in those days that our Chummy liked to sleep in the middle of the roadway in Norman Avenue, and if a car did come up the street he would look up and slope off to the side of the road before resuming his former slumbers. He wasn't disturbed very often.

My favoured form of transport to Leicester was by the old steam train with a clear signal ahead. In this image, it is heading away from Wigston station in the 1950s. (*Mike Mensing*)

elderly folks around me. My grandfather Lee's sister, Ada, had married a Peter Stokes, who turned out to be a wealthy shoemaker, and later a garage owner, in Bond Street, Leicester. They had several petrol stations and car dealerships in the Leicester area, and I believe, even today, that relatives on the Stokes side own one or more garages, although I would not know them now. When the old folks died out we lost touch, and even the younger generation then who remembered our family may have passed away by now, leaving a new generation behind with little or no knowledge of poor relatives by the name of Lee in Nuneaton.

It so happened that when my mum and dad got married, they were offered a house to rent in Norman Avenue, then lived in by my dad's uncle, Arthur Walsh. They moved in around 1937 and both my brother Jim, who was born in 1938, and myself, who was born in 1948, lived there with our parents. My mam and dad left Norman Avenue in 1968 and moved to Stockingford. Arthur Walsh was a Nuneaton postman for many years, but originally came from Leicester where he had married Granny Lee's sister – Auntie Maggie (Davis).

He retired in 1937 and wanted to return to his native Leicestershire, so the house in Norman Avenue became available and it was our family home for thirty years. Uncle Arthur and Auntie Maggie went to live in Glenfield (Sports Road), and I always remember that it was a particular thrill to visit this old couple (for me at any rate). They lived in a wooden bungalow and had an old railway carriage at the bottom of their garden. They had very primitive toilet arrangements too, a privy with a hole in a wooden plank over a cesspit.

Getting to Glenfield was an epic journey too. It took ages and involved some interesting means of transportation. First was the old steam train to Leicester. I dare say, when I look back over the years, my boyhood interest in steam trains stemmed from these journeys. Running into Leicester alongside the Midland main line, our little local train was overtaken by the fast expresses to St Pancras and long lumbering coal trains heading south or rattling empties going north. From time to time, Leicester station, with its dark overall roof, housed great steaming monsters as they pulled up with their trains. They fussed around shunting, hooking on and hooking off, and I took it all in. After all what other diversions did I have in my limited experience? I soaked up the sights and the atmosphere like a sponge. I remember those strange characters that inhabited the space between the platforms. They dodged the trains, but when they stopped went round banging the wheels of the carriages with a long handled hammer, or squeezed dangerously between the engine and the carriages, attaching and unattaching coaches. It was all most odd, risky, interesting and thrilling. Even to this day, I still like travelling by train because you are being taken on a ride. Travelling by car involves hard work. I drive but I am not an avid motorist. Give me a train and a bus any day! I love 'em.

I recall my dad telling me that Uncle Arthur had been a postman in Nuneaton for many years, and covered the villages the other side of the Watling Street from the Nuneaton delivery office. He used to get up before dawn and ride out by bike in all weathers (irrespective of torrential rain, snow, ice and freezing temperatures) to Higham on the Hill, Dadlington, Stoke Golding and round about. When he was off work ill, Auntie Maggie covered the round for him. Those were the days!

Other elderly relatives of Granny Lee whom I remember were my Auntie Jessie Davis and her companion, who was no relative but whom we affectionately called Auntie Foff. They were always welcome at our house. Another sister of my Granny was a striking character who dressed like a man. Auntie Ethel (Wells was her married name). I only vaguely remember Auntie Ethel's stern countenance, short, swept back, maybe Brylcreemed hair, horn-rimmed glasses

In the back garden at No. 52 Norman Avenue *c.* 1953 with our relatives: (back row) Uncle Arthur Walsh, married to Auntie Maggie, brother Jim, our Dad, Walter Lee. (Sitting) Auntie Jess from Leicester, Auntie Maggie from Sports Road, Glenfield, and me, Peter, with our Mam, Edna Lee, and Granny Lee. Auntie Jessie, Maggie and Granny Lee were sisters. We went to live in Uncle Arthur and Auntie Maggie's house in Norman Avenue when Uncle Arthur retired from the post office in 1937 and he moved to Glenfield. When Auntie Maggie died, Uncle Arthur went to live with his son, who kept a Boarding House in Penzance. We accompanied Granny Lee and Auntie Jessie, and her companion 'Auntie' Foff, to Skegness every Leicester holiday fortnight without fail, and sometimes we went at Easter too. I loved Skeggy. I still do in fact, for it has so many happy memories, although it is not everybody's idea of holiday heaven. I took myself there on my own (none of my family would dream of setting foot in the place!) a short while ago. It still has the magic for me, and more fish and chip shops than I could ever do justice to. The spirits of my long dead relations accompanied me on that visit.

and manly countenance. She wore a shirt and tie and smoked cigars! But I have no reason whatsoever to question her femininity. Her husband had been badly wounded in the First World War, and was an officer in the Army. He died early in the 1920s or '30s from his wartime injuries. Auntie Ethel was a herbalist by profession, and was assistant to a herbalist in Leicester city centre. When he died, she was left the business, which she carried on until she retired. I am not sure why we had less to do with Auntie Ethel. I got the impression she was thought to be a formidable character and therefore less fun. Her surviving photographs certainly enforce that opinion, but my father, particularly, never gave me the thought she was any less well thought of because of it. Certainly there was a little more distance with Auntie Ethel.

Auntie Jessie and Foff were very much liked. They were cheery characters and I looked forward to their regular visits. They usually came to us rather than our visiting them for some reason and I remember seeing them arrive carrying those old-fashioned suitcases, the sort you lugged through town from the station. You needed arms like Popeye in those days to carry luggage around.

Auntie Ethel.

There were no little wheels on suitcases like we have today. One or the other was, I remember, an accomplished pianist. We had an upright piano in our front room in Norman Avenue and Christmas was a happy time. It inevitably involved a visit from these two aunts and lots of lovely food, maybe even a chicken for Christmas lunch, and plenty of piano playing (Morecambe and Wise were way into the future in those days). The fact that Aunties Jess and Foff had never married was of no concern, when you think of the era they occupied; around the First World War, there was a shortage of healthy, young men after the carnage of the trenches. When whole generations of potential husbands were wiped out, it left a shortage of eligible men.

Skegness was 'Leicester on Sea' for two weeks of the year in late July and, being true to our roots, our relatives decamped to Skeggy for Leicester holiday fortnight. So did my parents, Aunties Jessie and Foff, and we stayed at the same bed and breakfast in Skegness year in year out. In fact, we sometimes went at Easter too. For the first fifteen years of my life, my regular summer holidays were spent at Catlin's guesthouse in Skeggy. We went there by Monty's bus.

Monty's buses were a Nuneaton institution. Particularly to those who lived on its domestic routes, Gipsy Lane, Bramcote and Caldwell. Their vehicles were mostly second-, third- or fourth-hand. I cannot imagine that Monty ever bought

A typical old Monty parked on waste ground opposite the garage in Attleborough Road, an area now covered by the Attleborough Arms.

Monty's Gipsy Lane service departs from the old Nuneaton bus station with its concrete shelters, erected in 1956. Imagine having to travel on one of these all the way to Skegness. The seats were not designed for long distances as I recall; they were decidedly hard on the bum!

new. They had a bedraggled livery of red and cream and chuntered along quite happily between the town centre and the local destinations mentioned above. From this point of view my family did not have a great deal of use for them, and my limited recall of a town trip on an old Monty only reminded me of a bus conductor with an impressive rack of different coloured card tickets, which on production of your few-coppers fare would induce the conductor to select the appropriate ticket and punch a hole in it with an interesting metal implement. This fascinated me as a kid. Fancy having put the money in a flappy and highly abraded leather pouch, and then fidgeting a ticket loose from an elongated mouse trap, which you then pierced with a lethal-looking punch. This routine was carried out not once but dozens of times a journey. What a fiddly job – it looked most satisfying! The problem was that our principal contacts with Monty's ancient buses were not on relatively uncomfortable but reasonably short local journeys, but on the run to Skegness. It was purgatory!

The only redeeming feature was the promise of a vast expanse of golden sands, and a mile-long promenade of funfairs, amusement stalls, abundant fish and chipperies, candy floss, sugary sticks of rock, messy treats, boating lakes and an exhilarating miniature railway ride. It took hours. Remember there were no dual carriageways in the '50s, and if you averaged 40 miles an hour you were doing very well indeed. One year, the inevitable happened and after a lot of crashing of gears we broke down in a village near Grantham. We ground to a stop and the driver set off to look for a red phone box. After a while he returned and told us another bus was being despatched from the Attleborough garage and that we had to wait until it arrived. Our sandwiches were eaten, our bladders became extended and general discomfort set in.

We arrived at Skeggy around seven hours after we had left Nuneaton. Half an hour later, we drank a nice cup of tea and a tiring day was forgotten. We couldn't say 'never again'. For us there was no other choice. It was old and clapped-out buses or nothing. Skeggy was that important!

I mentioned our little dog Chummy. I can never remember taking him for a walk. The animal was entirely independent of us apart from meal times of course, which kept him loyal. We just let him out when he scratched at the gate, and off he went. Several hours later he returned home for his supper. In the summer, he spent much of his time asleep in the centre of the road outside our house. There were so few cars in those days the roadway was empty. I suppose, thinking about it over the years, he carefully selected that spot because the centre of the road was always sunny despite the passing sun. It was a perfect suntrap and he loved it. I mentioned his little sausage dog girlfriend. She belonged to

On the beach at Skeggy. The couple on the left are Edna and Tom Orton, with their son Raymond from Nuneaton, friends of my parents. There's my dad, with little me on his lap aged about one, which dates this picture to around 1949/50. Behind my dad's deckchair is Lawrence Catlin's. His father owned a boarding house, which we stayed in for many years. Lawrence's dad, I recall, was involved in show business in Skeggy as an amateur compere of shows, and I recall that we once went to see a show he was in. There is my mam and our Jim on the right. Jim and Lawrence were pals and used to lark about together back then. I am not sure who took the photograph, possibly Granny Lee, who would meet up with our relatives. The old ladies I assume were engaged elsewhere in less lively activities.

one of the shops at the bottom of Norman Avenue on Queens Road. In my mind's eye, I think it might have been Porter's the ironmonger's on the corner of Edward Street, but I might be wrong. She too seemed to be independent and at times the two of them trotted around together quite amiably, sniffing trees and lamp posts, barking at other dogs and running towards cats. I suspect that if one of the cats had stood its ground, they would soon have retreated with their tails between their legs. They made a strange couple. Our little pooch, the type of mongrel that looked the same from both ends (so closely did he resemble a mop), and a classic Dachshund, smooth of hair, short of leg and with two beady eyes. There was no mistaking which way round she was. But as far as I know, there was no scandal in the family, no illicit offspring combining their two visual characteristics in the weirdest pups seen on Queens Road in the last century!

A regular visitor to our house was a lady called Mrs Clarke, a friend of Mam. Mrs Clarke loved dogs and she made a terrible fuss of our little Chummy. He responded well to the cooing and stroking, so much so that one day, in a fit of madness, my mother gave our Chummy to Mrs Clarke because she thought she loved him so much that it was only fair on the poor little mite to go to a good home like that. So off they set. Mrs Clarke led Chummy away with a lead on. I wasn't sure whether he wanted to go but I guess the new experience of being taken for a walk by this nice lady bemused him so much that off he

A picture of me.

trotted. Mrs Clarke lived in Richmond Road, not far from us but sufficiently far, we thought, for Chummy (whose only orbit had been Norman Avenue and the adjacent part of Queens Road) never to find his way home.

We were wrong. Several days later Chummy was heard scratching at the gate. When Mam let him in, she saw him peering at her through the mop of tousled hair with a look that said 'Don't you ever do that to me again!' She never did. Chummy remained a much loved yet almost entirely independent member of our family for the rest of his life.

Here is me aged eight or nine, I guess. Do you like the jumper? It was knitted by my mother. She knitted a lot of clothes for me. Even swimming trunks, but the less said about them the better. They only had one outing, you can imagine why. I still colour up with embarrassment thinking about it. So what did us lads do in the '50s with no television, computers, internet, electronic games or train sets? In the vernacular of the day, we 'mucked about'. I had a few pals who I mucked about with. Posh friends like Desmond Parker in Edward Street and the Everitts next door but one, in Norman Avenue. Desmond's dad was a chiropodist. There were four Everitt sons. Maurice, the oldest, was great pals with my brother Jim, Vince was a bit older than me, Wally the same age and Roy a bit younger.

School took up a lot of time but when we were not there our activities were solely dictated by the weather. If it was raining we stayed in, read comics, got bored and mythered our parents. If it wasn't raining or if it snowed we played outside.

As I recall, a few of the games were dreadful, but I was a kid. I pressed on way beyond the length of time when I should have known better and packed it in. Let's face it, there was not much choice. Marbles, for example ('Allis' we called them): perfect glass spheres with coloured interiors, which made me wonder how the colours got inside. I still have some at home because I couldn't bear to part with them and they don't take up much room. They remind me of the futile existence I used to lead. But as a game, they left a lot to be desired, mainly because you needed a flat, billiard-table surface to play on. We started off on the pavement or in our backyards, but paving slabs had the uncanny habit of being a poor playing surface. First of all the slabs weren't perfectly flat. The marbles had the infuriating habit of flying off sideways when they hit a joint in the paving. Some slabs were raised above the others or tilted. This annoyed us like mad, so we decided to play in the road. Remember there were few cars back then, and while my little dog Chummy lay there in the middle of the road sunning himself asleep and totally ignoring us, we kids were at the side trying to play marbles. Regrettably, road surfaces were almost as bad as paving. You had small stones, lumps, bumps and a camber to contend with. So we upgraded to big steel ball bearings ('Stunners' we called them). They were better at overcoming some of the obstacles, but the game still failed to live up to expectations. I am impressed at how we kept going for such a long time, undoubtedly because our choice of things to do was so limited.

Then there was conkers, another complete waste of time. In the conker season, armed with lumps of wood, we would seek out conker trees and fling our bits of wood into the branches to knock out the conkers. This job was frustrating because there were always some boys who had bigger bits of wood who stuck at it longer and knocked down bucket loads of conkers, whereas all we got were a couple of pocket fulls. These were sorted out into the biggest ones we could find. Of course the clever lads with the bigger chair legs got the biggest ones. By the odds stacked against us, they were bound to.

The game itself was less than satisfying. I do not know how some kids did it but their conkers seemed to be made of lead. They obviously had 'prepared' them in some way, perhaps cooking them in a gas oven. We only had a range and my conkers were only cooked where they had sat on the hot plate. The middle was still mushy. It's not surprising to find that I gave up after the first few games of having my conkers blasted apart after a few strikes. I can still remember the frustration. But the thought of standing there for hours on end hurling old chair legs into conker trees to prove how manly I was did not sit well with me. I moved on.

I mentioned the Everitts next door but one. They proved to be mischievous, a characteristic in a child much to my liking. Between our house and the Everitt's lived an elderly lady named May Mockford. She would have been of that generation of women whose choice of men was severely curtailed by the First World War. Her house, even in the 1950s, was a time warp. It was still lit by gas, and she had the biggest mangle I had ever seen. It was almost the height of her back kitchen ceiling and it frightened me. Those rollers looked so big and threatening, ready to mangle any young lads' appendages at a moment's notice.

Sometimes if I was out in the back garden messing about, Wally would stick his head over his wall and say 'fancy a muck raid?' This consisted of getting small lumps of soil and flinging them at each other in the knowledge if we did get hit, it would not do much damage. That was the theory at any rate. I found this pastime modestly satisfying, mainly because of the frisson of excitement that accompanied it: May, who lived in between, would spot the muck flying across her back garden (she was a very nosy neighbour) and we would hear her back door open. Wally would shout 'May's coming!' and we would fly in home, pretending to be innocent of all charges.

May's garden was given over almost entirely to the production of soft fruit, particularly rhubarb. It was the most splendid-looking rhubarb I have ever seen, and it grew in great profusion. May was very generous with her rhubarb too and we were given armfuls of it. We probably had rhubarb in various forms, in custard, in mixed fruit and in pies for dinner every day of the week. We always kept a goodly supply of May's rhubarb in our back shed. However, one day we stopped eating rhubarb. Mam had got into conversation with May and asked what the secret of great success with her rhubarb was. May replied that she always put the contents of her chamber pot on it! I often wondered if the blackened and wizened remains of May's last batch of rhubarb is still in the back shed of our old house in Norman Avenue today, forty-five years after we moved. Rhubarb was off the menu after that.

One day, I was returning home from some errand or other for my mam and turned out of Queens Road up the rise into Norman Avenue. I bumped into Wally Everitt (I think it was), trundling along an enormous filthy old pram. Interested to find out what he was up to, he responded that he was going down the gasworks to get some coke for his mam for the fire. For those who can remember, a feature of the town in those days was the premises of the Nuneaton Gas Company, whose gas holders, retorts, valves and other gubbins fizzled away in Queens Road day and night. The smell of coal gas production filled the air and was extremely pungent on some days, sometimes to the point of nausea. Unfortunately, under normal circumstances, gaining access to their yard to have a look round was barred to us kids, so I spotted an opportunity here and asked Wally if I could come along to help.

We set off to the gasworks. It wasn't as interesting as I had hoped. All you did was go through the gates, where you were confronted with a large pile of coke. You then had the horrible job of shovelling it into your favoured mode of transportation, a very large pot-bellied old pram on small wheels in our case. As you can imagine, I was blackened with dust from the coke. Visualise the scene as two filthy mawkins trundled the old pram up Queens Road, pushing it with great difficulty up the rise into Norman Avenue. Pram wheels wobbled and bent in all directions under the weight. Boy did I get into trouble with my mam when I got home!

# Chapter Two

# Messing About

I mentioned previously the poor games we played and the rough and ready ways we amused ourselves. Back in the '50s, we had a very big and interesting playground in the old town of Nuneaton. If you had asked me back then whether this was a great place to muck about in, I would not have known how to answer the question. You see, apart from Skegness (and Leicester where some relatives lived), Nuneaton was the only place I knew. Whereas Skeggy was glittery and summery with plenty of amusements, a great beach and one heck of a big paddling pool (the North Sea), Nuneaton was full of jitties, derelict old buildings, cut throughs and contraband materials you could use in your games. Let me give you some examples. As kids, we thought it very rakish if you could disappear down an entry (in Abbey Street, say) and emerge between the buildings in Queens Road. It gave us a sense of one-upmanship. Here are all these adults pootling along, not knowing that that entry leads down there and comes out over there. While they have to walk round the streets, us kids could whizz through and come out way over in the distance. If, on the odd occasion, someone you had just seen in Abbey Street suddenly saw you as he or she turned into Queens Road ahead of them, he or she would think 'how did that little bugger get past me, I didn't see him!' You could see the quizzical look on their faces. An offshoot of this predilection for jitties was a game we played in the winter months when it was dark. We used to go 'hedge hopping'.

In Norman Avenue, where we lived, all the houses had small front gardens, most with straggly privet hedges in them (that is if they had a hedge at all). The idea was to start at one end of the street, two at a time, and creep sneakily through each front garden over the entry to the next before finally nipping down an entry at the end and over a wall into the grounds of the old Primitive Methodist chapel on the corner of Edward Street and Queens Road. There

Abbey Street in the 1950s.

The market place, 1951.

were no fixed rules other than to remain entirely undetected (or told off by any of the residents of the houses whose front gardens you were trespassing in). Also, we tried to avoid tearing our clothes on bits of metal, twigs or other obstacles, otherwise our Mams would give us a good telling off. Most people in those days only used their front rooms for best occasions. For a start, they usually only kept one fire going and that was in the back parlour, so for most of the year the front room was cold and dark. There was little danger of being seen. But sometimes, very rarely, someone had lit the fire in the front hearth and had people round. The curtains had been left open. This meant that we had to crawl on our bellies under the window sill before creeping over the wall across the entry over the next wall and so on. This got our adrenalin pumping a bit, and we were sorely relieved when we passed that particular house without detection. A few of the walls were as tall as we were and took some scaling, but that was part of the fun. It was quite a convoluted journey to reach the end of the street and we then dashed through an entry at the end, down a back garden and clambered over the back wall into the grounds of the Primitive Methodist church, which stood on the corner of Queens Road and Edward Street.

Remains of an old court cottage (on the right). This was typical of old Nuneaton town. (*Peter Lee*)

Abbey Street was full of backyards, jitties, alleyways and outhouses. The buildings we see here were old weaving top shop workrooms. Some of these were our playground, which we explored looking for bric-a-brac. (*Peter Lee*)

Queens Road in the 1920s. The buildings on the right did not change much in the 1950s.

Old Abbey Street at night. The lighted building in the centre of the picture marks Meadow Street before Abbey Street changes to Upper Abbey Street.

This all went wrong one night when, as we tiptoed down the last back garden, some old bloke rushed out and started shouting at us. We skedaddled over that back wall like a streak of lightning, except that instead of our usual caution, which brought us to a delicate landing in the Prims' yard, on this occasion there was an almighty clatter, and this triggered all the local dogs in the vicinity in a cacophony of barking. In the process of clambering over the back wall, instead of my usual carefully considered descent to the other side, I dropped down quickly and shoved one foot in a bucket of dirty water. In a panic, I wondered how it had got there, but seeing my pal disappearing into the distance I withdrew my soaked foot and fled squelching after him. We regrouped at the entrance to the Prims' frontage and peered around the gate. We thought it unwise to return into Norman Avenue to go back home that way directly in case the old bloke we had upset, anticipating this, was lurking about waiting for us. Instead, we went the long way round and sloped off up Edward Street and round Princes Street into Norman Avenue. With one damp leg and my left pump full of water, I squelched all the way.

Hedge hopping lost its attraction for a while, but one day my mates suggested we give it another go and we agreed to meet as usual that night at the jump off point. On this occasion I took precautions and wore Wellington boots instead of wearing my usually lightweight and decidedly nifty pumps, remembering the potential for getting my feet wet. The evening started badly. Those Wellington boots made so much noise clumping along that the others refused to let me come along with them – I was 'too damned noisy' (or words to that effect), so I retired home, left them to it, and never went hedge hopping again. It had entirely lost its appeal.

Another facet of the town back then was the high number of derelict buildings around. In the '50s, Nuneaton was a scruffy place and many of the houses, in Abbey Street particularly, were regarded as slums. Many were without proper sanitation, had mediocre running water, and were cramped, poorly lit and dirty. We sometimes ventured into these old properties, creeping through their

Abbey Street. One of Reg. Bull's photographs from 1951. A few years before I was actively exploring the town with my mates. By the time I took interest in the mid- to late '50s most of these properties were ready for demolition, but behind them were dozens of old cottages, yards, jitties, and alleyways, which we ran through knowing that the former residents – now departed – could not take umbrage at our presence as they had done formerly. The only danger was tramps using unused tenements as temporary lodgings. These old premises were a good hunting ground for kids looking for old prams, bits of wood, rope or anything else we could get our hands on that could be turned to some practical use.

*Above:* the Primitive Methodist chapel stood on the corner of Queens Road and Edward Street. It was an elaborate building and we knew every inch of it. On that fateful hedge-hopping night, when we were forced to run for it, we emerged from the right-hand side of the chapel where there was a backyard and fled through the sidegate on the left fronting Edward Street. (*Reg. Bull, Ruby Atkins Collection*)

*Right:* Little girls in my group of pals, including my favourite Carol (top left). I'm in the middle row on the right. The other kids are (bottom row) Yvonne (Vonny) Duell, Desma Melbourne, (middle) Geoff Melbourne, me, (top) Carol Burton and Chris Melbourne. I think we must all have been out on a Sunday trip in Jack Melbourne's Dormobile.

open doors and having a quick look around to see if there was anything we could use in our games. Old chair legs were particularly prized for a very short time, as they were the right size and weight for knocking conkers out of trees. But very often these houses were totally devoid of interest. We never ventured upstairs, as we were worried that a bedroom might house a slumbering tramp. The trouble was that the only means of egress was a steep narrow set of stairs, which might make you a perfect target for a heavy flying object like a beer bottle. So we were wise enough never to go up stairs in these old places.

There was one incident though that I look back on now with acute embarrassment. The council were demolishing old Church Street, so I guess this might have been around 1959/60 when I was eleven or twelve. As the properties were prepared for demolition, we did our usual reconnaissance to ascertain if there was anything we could appropriate to play with. There was an old car repair garage in Church Street and our eyes fell upon a pair of filthy, old oil drums. We realised that, lashed together with a few planks on top, this would make a great raft for the canal. So we rolled the barrels home, got hold of some old floor boards and a quantity of rope (probably lifted from one of these old buildings) and set to making a 'raft'. On completion, we carried this contraption up Norman Avenue, along Princes Street, across the 'Patch' and up the jitty to the Cat Gallows Bridge. Just by the bridge we launched our raft and clambered on. Immediately upon boarding the raft, a distinctive glugging noise was to be heard. We scrambled off to watch our raft slowly sinking. We had forgotten that in the ends of the oil drums were bung holes and these were, of course, open. The water got in and the raft was doomed. I expect it's still there on the bottom of the cut, just below the Cat Gallows Bridge, to this day.

# Chapter Three

# Girls

Little girls my age were alien creatures to me. I met quite a few at school of course, but I did not play with them. For all I knew, they might have come from Venus (or Bedworth), so far apart were our interests in life. They played with dolls, went to dancing classes and looked fresh and clean in their little frocks. I mucked about with my mates, played football in the playground, and by the end of the day was thoroughly dishevelled with scratches on my knees and dirty hands.

I recall one incident in school. I was caught talking to one of the pals I sat next to in class by a particularly viperous teacher who had famously and publicly admitted that she hated children. This horrible teacher – and I will never forgive her for this – summoned me to the front of the class and made me go and sit next to a girl. A girl! I would not have been more embarrassed if she had stood me facing the wall with a pointed hat on and the letter D painted on the front. As I sat down, I could hear the other lads tittering and, as I furtively looked round, I saw them sniggering and pulling faces. It was truly awful.

I remember another incident. One day, I was at home and (I can't remember how I fell for this one) was persuaded by my mam to go with her to a friend's house up the road for a cup of tea. I have tried to think how it came about, maybe I had been found guilty of some misdemeanour or other, or perhaps my usual mates were not at home and, having no one to play with, my mother felt it appropriate not to leave me in the house on my own. On reflection, the weight of evidence suggests I would have been beholden to my mam for a bout of naughtiness for which I had to do penance. I knew when I got to our destination that there would follow a sea of solid nattering only relieved by a glass of pop and hopefully a plate of biscuits. But it was worse. Much worse! When we got there I was pitched out into the yard to play with this lady's little girl! Words cannot describe the horror, and then it got worse still. Instead of being sweet and demure, this little girl had the hauteur of Boadicea. She led me to a line of three orange boxes she had carefully arranged on her backyard and peremptorily told me that she and I were going to play trains! I assume her mam had said play trains with Peter when he comes round, 'cos he likes trains', and this was her idea of playing trains. That we had to sit on these boxes and imagine we were on a train and make choo-choo noises. The very thought froze the blood in my veins. It was beyond awful. But, of course, it soon occurred to this little girl that statically sitting there for just a few minutes and an exhaustive bout of 'Toot Toot' and 'Choo Choo' was as much as one could sustain without the whole exercise feeling a bit limited in its scope. As she suspended her former stern demeanour, I fled indoors and possibly had words with my mam. I am not sure whether these words were totally effective, but I was never asked to repeat the exercise and my mother did not invite me to tea around her friend's again. I assume that if she needed to leave me in the house to go out for a good natter she felt comfortable in doing so, in the knowledge that I was sensible enough not to set the house on fire or flood the kitchen.

There was, though, a little girl I did have a soft spot for. She was blonde, soft and pretty, looking in my mind's eye like a fairy as she trotted to school on the opposite side of the road to me in Norman Avenue. I went to Fitton Street School and she went in the opposite direction (I can only assume she went to Queens Road School). The fact she went to an unknown school must have amplified the affection. Of course, I would never cross the road to say hello to her. I was much too shy. And even if our paths had crossed, the encounter would have induced my face to go a pale shade of beetroot to the roots of my ears. Better not to risk it. So I glanced furtively as she trotted to school on her side of the road and I trudged along in the opposite direction on my side.

Then one day she was seen no more. She vanished from her usual walk to school on the opposite side of the road. I assumed at first she had been taken on her holidays by her parents, but two weeks went by and she did not return to her former route. Weeks went by and I never saw her again. I was devastated. I questioned my mam furtively about this, in the hope of not giving her a clue as to a possibly embarrassing crush, and was surprised that my mother, knowing her propensity for gossiping, knew very little about the family other than that they had moved to another area of town. That solved the mystery, and I clung to the hope for a while of seeing my little fairy in the town one day, but I never saw her again – not even later in my teenage years, when we used to go to the Co-op hall and I could call on reserves of Dutch courage to talk to girls. It was very strange, but, to this day, I still have this vision in my mind's eye of this little fairy-like creature trotting down Norman Avenue on a warm summer's day, looking blonde, soft and radiant in her pretty dress. It's all very sad really, but if I did chance to meet her now it would never be the same. We would both be disappointed.

There was also a girl in our street who was also to my liking. Her name was Carol and she lived with her mum, who everyone in our family called Auntie Kate. We were close, but not remotely related. Carol was a few years older than me, cute, dimply and cheeky, and Auntie Kate was a surrogate mother to me at times. She would even take me to the clinic for my inoculations and other school kid checkups if Mam was at work. Auntie Kate's house was a destination my mam could take me to, even if I knew that, once there, the two would dissolve into a sea of prattle. Carol, who was that much older, had her own circle of friends of course, as well as being a girl and doing girly things, so we did not hang around together in that sense, but I never felt any embarrassment at all with her.

# Chapter Four

# Keeping Clean Against the Odds

The kitchen in the photograph opposite is not our kitchen, I hasten to add, but is perhaps typical of the kitchens in many of the old cottages and terraced houses in Nuneaton in the '50s. In our house we did have a white Belfast sink, a cold tap, a plastic bowl and a bottle of California Syrup of Figs on the mantelpiece. But our kitchen was much less grotty than this one. As I recall, it was clean, nicely painted and my mother had a stretched wire under the sink with a pleasant curtain hanging from it to hide the packets of 'OMO' and stocks of soap, bottles of Dettol, a hand brush and pan and other kitchen accoutrements. When I was a kid, my mam sent me out bright and well scrubbed every morning. How she did it under the circumstances is hard to imagine today.

Back in the 1950s, half the houses in Nuneaton had bathrooms, hot and cold running water, and inside toilets. The other half had no bathroom, an outside loo and one cold tap over a Belfast sink. Our house in Norman Avenue fell into the latter category. Despite this, our Mam started me off in the morning well scrubbed and clean. Although I began the day clean, I dare say my general appearance deteriorated as the day progressed. I cannot ever remember any kid in my class being smelly through poor hygiene though, but I do recall how easy it was for us lads to look dishevelled, like we'd been 'dragged through a hedge backwards', as my mam would say. Collars awry, shirt hanging out, socks down around our ankles, dirty scuffed knees. It was a badge of honour to sport a big scab on our knees. There was something satisfying about a spent scab that could be picked off, leaving the fresh pink skin underneath. Picking scabs was a great pleasure of mine at the time. After all, you had to take your fun in small doses in the '50s, as it was so few and far between. It was akin to the pleasure we had later on squeezing zits in our teenage years.

My mother achieved my state of morning cleanliness by being highly organised. Every day we had a goodly supply of hot water from a big kettle,

Kitchen sink, complete with leaky tap.

and most days we had a copper in our back kitchen full of hot water, which she used for washing our clothes and also as a source of water for bathing. Every day was the same routine. Mam had taught us how to cleanse every orifice of our bodies with the use of a generous flannel. The flannel she used was enormous, the size of a hand towel. This use of a big flannel was superbly efficient in scouring our body parts and leaving them freshly presented for the day. On Friday nights, we had our weekly bath using an old zinc bath that hung in the wooden shed at the back of the house. The soap we used was a particularly pungent variety I remember. Carbolic is a word that springs to mind, but it was more likely to be Wrights Coal Tar or Pears, as Carbolic might have brought my delicate epidermis out in a rash. By this simple routine we stayed clean. It was laborious, hard work but it did the job. My reward on Saturday, after a Friday night bath, was to wear a best clean shirt and be allowed to go to the Saturday matinee at the Ritz. All us kids went there; it was the place to be on Saturday mornings and the highlight of our week. We had to be well turned out too. There were little girls in the audience! All through her life my mam was the model of cleanliness, and she always left home and went into the street well groomed. She knew a lot of people and she was very particular about her appearance, after all, once she emerged into the roadway it would not be long until she would see somebody she knew and strike up a conversation, and heaven forbid they would be distracted by any sloppy lack of dress sense or presentation. I can hear my mother tut-tutting now if old Mrs so-and-so was less than neatly turned out in the dress department. I recall clashing colours being a bit of a gripe with my mother. In fact, it rubbed off on me a bit. My mam and dad, although not terribly well off, could afford to buy new clothes and visited the Co-op on a fairly regular basis. Maybe J. C. Smith's too, but I suspect my parents preferred the Co-op because of the 'Divvy'.

# Chapter Five

# Fun and Frolics

Demarcation lines and territories were quite important in the '50s. I seemed to stick to my side of Norman Avenue, whereas there were kids on the other side I never played with. I knew them by sight of course and sometimes talked to them in the playground at school, but we never played together in the street. It's strange but I still can detect how I felt about the other side of the road in Norman Avenue. It was foreign territory. I felt uncomfortable if I was 'over there', yet my own side was familiar and comfy. I can remember lots about the kids on my side of the road but virtually nothing about those over the other. Thinking about it now there were very few kids who were my everyday playmates anyway, and it seemed to amount to one family: the Everitts.

Occasionally we would be encroached on by a little lad who lived down the road, but we did not like playing with him. He unsettled us. He was quite literally the moistest drip you could imagine. He always seemed to have two green, runny candles hanging from his nostrils, which he dealt with in the most disturbing fashion possible. He would either sniff constantly or, if the candles overwhelmed his sniffing and reach his lips, he would poke his tongue out and sweep it across his top lip to remove the offending build up. What we couldn't understand was that no matter what time of year it was, winter or summer, he sported these candles. He always seemed to have a streaming cold although there were no other cold-like symptoms. We only needed to study this for a short time to realise this was not a kid to be played with. The candles, the constant sniffing and licking grossed us out. We could not understand why his Mam did not issue him with a handkerchief. But, looking back now, in view of the deficiencies in the laundry department of the '50s, it was probably less time consuming for his mother to wash his dribbled-on jersey occasionally than a whole bunch of stiff handkerchiefs every week. Needless to say, as soon as he poked his head round, we skedaddled. No matter what we were doing, playing marbles, hop scotch, pushing our Dinky Toys round the pavement, his appearance caused us to sweep all our stuff up and leg it up the road as fast as we could go. I have never had an urge to escape so fast before or since. We did not dash in home for fear of his calling on us and we would be trapped into playing with him. Distance was the most important thing.

While exploring the yards and jitties of the old town for junk, our most prized and looked for acquisition was an old pram, or more importantly pram wheels. Equipped with these we could move up into a whole new dimension of mobility. Back in the '50s trolleys were all the fashion. These were all bespoke contraptions, cobbled together from whatever pieces of wood and rope you could find. But above all you needed wheels, and derelict prams were very hard to come across, particularly those with a decent set of wheels. Very often we would find a pram body without wheels, as they had been robbed by somebody before we got to them, or the axles were bent, or the spokes were buckled, or so rusty as to be ready to fall apart as soon as any stress was put on them. So it was with great relish that we fell on an old pram with a decent set of wheels. For some reason, I did very well and had a set of wheels from two prams, small at the front and large at the back. This was the best kind of trolley, and very nifty indeed. Kitted out with a decent undercarriage, I set to and made a trolley, using discarded bits of wood raided from derelict houses and a lot of ingenuity. I remember wanting to give it an even slicker image and foraging in our shed for some paint. All I could find that had not already set hard with age was an old tin of emulsion my dad had used to paint the thrawl in the pantry. It was a rather insipid shade of pea green. Nevertheless, it was destined to transform my trolley, in my eyes at least. I am not sure what my pals thought of it! I can't remember their comments. At first, careering around the street on a trolley was good fun, except of course when I fell off, which I did frequently, and produced a good crop of scabs on my knees. I buzzed pedestrians and domestic animals, and used the hill down Norman Avenue into Queens Road to get up a fair lick of speed. That is until I was roundly told off one day by a policeman for endangering the public. This kind of put a dampener on it and I wondered how I could still extract some more fun out of my trolley and stay within the law. One day, I had brainwave and took it on myself to give trolley rides, halfpenny a go. At first there were no takers, until one day a little girl who lived nearby was persuaded to part with a halfpenny and I gave her a complete tour around the block. She was so taken with it she went in home and came back with another halfpenny. So we did it again. She must have parted with the whole of tuppence when her mother came out and remonstrated with me for diddling her daughter out of all this money! So that was the end of trolley rides. I kept the trolley a while longer before my mam and dad bought me a brand new push bike and the trolley was promptly abandoned in the shed. It may still be there for all I know.

Old pram wheels were a precious commodity in 1950s Nuneaton.

# Chapter Six

# Getting Started in Local History

When I was a kid in Nuneaton town I never heard the words 'local history' banded about, so I was gloriously ignorant of the finer points of what I was ultimately to let myself in for. I just mucked about with my pals and the old town unfolded before me. There was one clearly defined moment though which has always stuck in my mind. It lit a bright lamp in my childish head that something was quite special about Nuneaton, and kindled something in me that has stayed ever since.

One day, when I could only have been five or six years old, my parents took me on a walk to Collycroft to see a very elderly aunt (by the name of Letts). She was an ancient Victorian lady dressed in black who inhabited a dingy terraced house somewhere near the 'Bottom River'. Usually, my parents would catch a Midland Red bus in Coton Road, but as this was a particularly fine summer's day they decided to walk, and I did not really mind. I trotted out with them happily enough. Up until that time, I had only ever played outside in the street, gone to Fitton Street school and accompanied my parents or my granny into town on a Saturday, so the only landscapes I knew then were terraced streets, shops, and, of course, the odd trip to Leicester to see relatives on the train or our annual holiday outing to Skeggy.

One thing I thought about this excursion, though, was that my parents were taking me 'a funny way'. We marched up Princes Street, across the Patch and through the Jitty, which took us up to the 'Cat Gallows' bridge over the canal. At that point I entered another world. The canal, and as we crossed the bridge a panorama of the town, opened up like something I had never seen before. But it got better, much better. Beyond the 'Cat Gallows' bridge we crossed Greenmoor Road and I observed a strange moonscape of clay banks, ponds interlaced with bushes and trees and distant, tall chimneys like some kind of

Remember the Maypole?

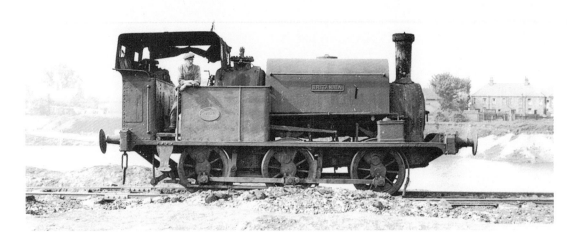

Still to be seen at Griff collieries in the 1950s. This old locomotive was named *Britannia*.

The Bermuda Arm of the Coventry Canal. (*Geoff Edmands*)

Newdigate Square.

Bermuda Village.

foreign land. 'The Cloddies' would soon be a wonderful playground for me and my mates but here I was seeing it for the first time.

Then we headed up Bermuda Road. Here was another sensation. Strangely grim, blackened and clanking buildings, and behind them a steaming, fiery volcano. Griff No. 4 Colliery with its burning pit tip. I was overwhelmed. This was exciting. We plodded on.

Soon there was more to see. On the right, more black and grimy buildings, a brickyard and railway trucks and sidings just visible among the sheds. There was a big pit on the left with black water in it. Then we entered a strange and quaint looking street 'Bermuda Village'. At the end was a level crossing with more railway trucks, a line of rails curving away in both directions, points going off different ways and numerous sidings.

We crossed the railway and to our left was a canal basin with several boats moored up, and another sunken below the water line. Way across the fields was another set of black sheds, smoky chimneys and queer looking buildings – Griff Clara Colliery. We then entered a lovely wooded walk as we turned down towards Collycroft and through Griff. It was all a magical mystery tour, and I

Griff Colliery Tip.

An aerial view taken in the 1960s when new housing was starting to encroach on our kiddy playground. The Cloddies is in the centre of the photograph. (*Geoff Edmands*)

remember it now as though it was yesterday, so firmly did it stick in my mind.

Later on, of course, I became blasé about it. The Cloddies were to feature a great deal in my expeditions to play Cowboys and Indians with my mates, or to catch any unspecified small animal we could get our hands on to take home as pets; sticklebacks, frog spawn and tadpoles were popular, and we kept them in a gold fishbowl until they all seemed to die prematurely. It had a super abundance too of narrow gullies, defiles and declivities, hidden behind shrubs and bushes where we could play hide-and-seek, and rusty railway tracks that looped around derelict buildings. There was an abundance of old pipes, which could be used as dangerous bridges to cross gullies. We didn't seem to bother about the inherent dangers in what we were doing, and our parents didn't seem to mind either. I do recall sometimes having sweaty nightmares where I dreamt about scaling clay pit sides, as I used to do, with their inevitable, dangerous blue ponds at the bottom and the sides giving way like an avalanche. It never happened to me in real life, but I scared myself with the thought of it once or twice in the dead of night.

Over the years, what I never seemed to understand was only ever meeting a few people who were really interested in the things I saw then, and knew much about the history of it all. Those that did, Geoff Edmands, Mick Lee (no relation), Alan Cook, Maurice Billington, Vic Holloway and Fred Phillips, became firm and wonderful friends in later years, but when I was a kid, my aroused curiosity was unsated.

For the time being then, I could not be classified as a budding 'local historian', and I rail against that description now. In my opinion, there is something 'naff' about the title. All I am is interested in where I live, and I have looked into it in a bit more detail than most. I honestly do not know why I possess this interest. I could easily have gone into football, or trains, or cars, or a thousand other 'manly' interests, but for some reason this curiosity about my home district stayed with me, and has got stronger over the years. It all stemmed from that trip to Collycroft one sunny and glorious day in the mid-1950s. In later years, the more I have learned the more I have wanted to know, and there is so much more to know about Old Nuneaton.

# Chapter Seven

# School, Courtaulds and Me

I went to Fitton Street school as a kid. Some of the other children in our street went to Queens Road but I never knew why. Those that did I hardly came into contact with. For some reason, I seem not to be able to remember much about school. Fitton Street must have made an impression, as I managed to get through my eleven-plus and go to Manor Park Grammar School. A few things come to mind. My school day started with the familiar chime of Courtaulds clock, which was only three streets away, its bell striking eight with a sonorous dong. I was thoroughly flannelled by my mam at the sink. I always remember she paid special attention to my neck area, rubbing it vigorously. She hated to see dirty necks and collars, and often mentioned it if she saw kids out like that. Somehow, and I don't know why, little boys had a predilection for an accretion of dirt, which seemed always to form a ring around the neck. A veritable high watermark of muck! Every time I have a shower or bath today I think about my mother's attention to detail in that area, and feel somehow that my extra vigorous application of soap in that region of the body is due to her unseen supervision from another dimension. I cannot recall what we ate for breakfast but I must have been well fed. My family never stinted on food. Then, at around a quarter to nine, I would head off in the direction of school.

I only have dim memories of school. That horrible, viperous, stick insect teacher who famously admitted she hated children. The other teachers were kind but firm, without being vicious, so much so that none come to mind. I could not have been marked out by any of them for special treatment, in which case I would have remembered.

The rest of my schooldays are a fog. I remember playing football in the playground, and a brief stint at conkers that was a complete waste of time. I remember it was all the rage for a brief period until it suddenly occurred to everyone how pointless conkers were. The game was promptly abandoned by all the lads in the playground except the one who had the hardest conker. We thought he had moulded a lump of lead to the shape of a conker then painted it brown. We played tig, threw balls, cricket, and I always remember one lad who could literally pee over the boys urinal wall into the garden beyond. We always thought it was a neat thing to do, but nobody else could seem to achieve the necessary trajectory or velocity, try as we might. It was a wonder at the time.

One day, a few years ago, I received a phone call from a kid with whom I went to school at Fitton Street. As you could imagine, I had not seen him since around 1960, so it was quite a surprise. He was now living in Torquay but was coming up to Nuneaton to visit some relatives, and wondered if I fancied going out for a beer. We did, and it was amazing that he could remember a lot of things that had been completely erased from my memory – names of teachers, fellow pupils and incidents. He gave me a photocopy of a piece of paper I had given to him with a Sputnik I had drawn on it. I was surprised, for I had totally forgotten how interested I was in space travel back then. Then, memories started to trickle back into my mind. I eagerly read the comic

Courtaulds always seemed to be a dramatic edifice. Its majestic bulk rose above the town and surprised you with its sudden appearance.

Courtaulds Mill at night. A billion clicks a second from the rayon machines working on all those floors created an amazing wall of sound. The chimes of the clock regulated our lives. (*W. H. Pope, courtesy Colin Yorke*)

Courtaulds, just before demolition.

Courtaulds sailed on a sea of rooftops.

As you travelled around the town, Courtaulds (in the centre of the picture on the horizon) would hove into view. It gave the mill a strange, ethereal aspect, which comforted local people. When Courtaulds was seen on the skyline you knew you were back in Nuneaton. This photograph was taken in the 1980s but it illustrates the point.

The Co-op, as built in the 1930s.

The Co-op in the 1950s. The grocery department was on the left-hand side, and the men's tailoring department on the right.

I bought every week – the *Eagle,* published in the '50s – from cover to cover. We forget these days that this period was the height of the Cold War and the Russians were ahead in the space race. We were both fearful and interested at the same time. If a third world war broke out, it was no good hiding in our Anderson shelter at the bottom of the garden. More substantial tunnels were needed and I knew where there was one – over the Cloddies. I have been modestly, but not overwhelmingly, interested in space ever since, and always wondered what it would be like to be captured by aliens. I did not have far to look, they were all around me, but I had hardly noticed them – girls! And I have since been captured on a number of occasions, though not always with favourable results.

After a full school day, which was regulated by the chimes of Courtaulds clock, I waited to hear the chimes of its deep sounding bell when the afternoon came. It chimed two, three times, then it was time to go home. I cannot tell you how much I looked forward to the school going home bell and, despite nice lessons in the afternoon such as art, the pull of home time seemed to me an eternity away.

When my Granny Lee was alive, I used to rush from school and go to the steps of Courtaulds canteen where she worked. I met her when she left for the afternoon and we walked home together. Something sticks in my mind today, as fresh as it did back in 1955 – the sound of Courtaulds factory. It was the most fantastic sound I had ever heard. The building shook with a million clicks a second and all the weaving machinery inside shuttled rayon backwards and forwards. It was a truly amazing wall of noise. I loved Courtaulds factory, there was something uncommonly friendly about it. My mam worked there as a youngster until she got married. My Granny Lee kind of arranged the marriage, as she told my dad that there was a particularly nice young lady who came in the canteen who was footloose and fancy free. She offered to introduce them both if he hung about about outside the factory. But my mam was not initially impressed. She was a good-looking girl and had other suitors, but somehow Granny Lee swung it. I think my mother saw in her a surrogate mother my mam had never had (she was abandoned as a youngster), and Granny and my dad were a better package than that which was on offer elsewhere. She not only got a loving husband but a warm-hearted and cheery new mother, who was an excellent cook. Granny Lee was the main cook in our household until she died in 1957, and I can still remember her lovely roast Sunday dinners and her insistence on having fish on Fridays without fail.

My mam left Courtaulds when she got married. She had to, because they did not employ married women back then. Had you been a man at the time,

Courtaulds must have been a dream job, surrounded by hundreds of unmarried young ladies all eager for a man!

My connection to Courtaulds goes back further though, since my grandfather James Walter Lee (1883–1927) came from Leicester to Nuneaton specifically to work on the construction of Courtaulds factory in 1914, just as the site was being prepared in readiness for construction. Then, of course, the First World War broke out, which slowed the work down considerably (Courtaulds was completed in 1921) as so many skilled artisans volunteered, as did my grandfather. He ended up in the Northumberland Regiment, presumably to fill the gaps in their ranks after the debacle of 1916 when men from all over the country, irrespective of origin, plugged holes in regiments that had been decimated. My grandfather died prematurely in 1927 when he fell off his bike when the wheel caught in a tramline along the tram route to Coventry. While getting over his injuries he caught pneumonia and died. These tragedies were very common back then. At the age of fourteen, my dad, who was the only son, was an orphan, and he and Granny Lee had to scrimp as best they could in their terraced house in Nuneaton, but the Leicester Lee and Davis families rallied round in a big network of support. One Leicester uncle paid for my mam and dad's wedding. Back then, we were a very close family, despite not being able to communicate regularly other than by letter or postcard.

Another thing I liked about Courtaulds was its lovely colour, created by those beautiful, soft, pink bricks (by Webster Hemmings in Coventry). On a warm summer's day the factory glowed with radiant heat. In addition, I was fascinated by how the clock tower seemed to pop up in various parts of the town. You would round a corner and see it through gaps in the houses, or as you descended into town from Stockingford on the Midland Red bus, or on the Leicester Road Bridge returning from Leicester, or cresting Hill Top. The mill rose above the town like a stately galleon floating on a sea of roof tops.

Then there was the clock. That too had a magical, ethereal appeal. You could be somewhere on the fringes of town, walking along, and suddenly you would hear the familiar chimes of Courtaulds in the distance, depending which way the wind was blowing, like some ghost clock. If you were not familiar with the district, it might seem odd to hear the distant chimes, but to me it was strangely comforting. I lived the first twenty years of my life in close proximity to that sound. It regulated my life when I was a school kid and I miss it. I believe the town was better then.

# Chapter Eight

# Food and Drink

Back in the '50s, we were very unsophisticated in our eating habits. We had to be, there was nothing else. No curries, no pizzas, no kebabs, no spaghetti, no lasagne, or pasta of any kind, no rice, Chinese or Indian Food, no chilli con carne. They had never been heard of in old Nuneaton, or some perhaps even invented back then. But the food we did have was just as eye-poppingly flavoursome compared with what we eat today. I'll give you an example. A great treat for me was when my mam or Granny Lee took me into town on a Saturday morning to get our groceries for the weekend. You shopped fresh and the idea was to make our way along to the market place and buy the vegetables for the Sunday roast (a long job because my mam and granny had a lot of nattering acquaintances). On the way, we stopped off at Coggans the baker's, and stepped into their wonderful shop with that gorgeous fragrance of fresh cakes and newly baked bread that soaked the atmosphere. On entry, there was a gentle chorus of 'oohs' and 'aahs', the look of pleasure (and glint in the eye) on shoppers' faces, which lit up at the sight of the lovely selection of toothsome cakes that lay before them. We drooled over cream cakes, carefully selecting one each to go with our cup of tea in the afternoon. Without fail, we always bought a large cottage loaf, the sort where there was a smaller round section of loaf on top of a larger base. Coggans baked the most heavenly cottage loaves in the universe! When we got home at lunchtime we fell upon that loaf and tore it to pieces like wild animals, smothering it with real butter. We consumed it with a passion, and I have never seen bread eaten like it since. The loaf seem to disappear in seconds, and that was our Saturday dinner. It was wonderful.

On the subject of bread, we always had ours delivered by the Co-op bakery delivery man. We bought bread checks from the Co-op grocery on the corner of Queens Road and the High Street and gave them to the delivery man when he came round with a rectangular wicker basket on his arm so my mam could

Nuneaton market, 1930s. Things had not changed much in the 1950s.

make a selection. I can even remember the time when the bread van was drawn by a horse! The delivery chap was not allowed to carry cash. It had to be bread checks. It was a complicated system I thought, but my mam did it for years. I remember the delivery man too – a very mild-mannered and retiring sort of chap. I cannot remember his name though. I think he was so retiring that even my mother, with her notable talents for passing the time of day, could not engage him much in conversation.

On the other hand, our milkman was an entirely different kettle of fish. His name was Aubrey Barnes and he was an archetypal milkman. I always thought being a milkman was a lonely lifestyle. We occasionally heard the chink of milk bottles at some ungodly hour, five o'clock in the morning maybe, and knew that Aubrey was abroad. He called around on Saturday for his money. He was a self-employed milkman, not from the Co-op, but I think I remember he obtained his bulk supplies from the Co-op Dairy in Merevale Avenue anyway. Aubrey was said to be a ladies' man, although he never married (as far as I know). When he presented himself on our back doorstep, he knocked then always shouted out a silly ditty. I can't remember the exact wording but it went something like this, 'A shilling, a bob, two and six's half a crown, a tanner aint!', or words to that effect. My mam was smitten with Aubrey and scurried to the door with the milk money. She was happily engaged by him in silly prattle for quite a few minutes. You could see why he was a ladies' man because he had the perfect level of daft banter ladies liked. My dad and I both cringed as Aubrey nattered away and my mam loved it. I often thought Aubrey was the only man my mam would run off with! We were startled one day when he turned up looking impeccable in a black suit, white shirt and dickey bow. He was off to some dinner or other that evening but did his collection dressed ready. He must have charmed his lady customers out of the trees. I wonder if Aubrey is still my mam's milkman as he performs his milk round in old Nuneaton in the sky!

We bought our meat fresh from Jack Melbourne's butcher's in Queens Road. Jack was a personal family friend of ours, and we even had the honour of being taken out by Jack and Betty Melbourne with their kids in Jack's Bedford Dormobile on a Sunday on a fairly regular basis. It was great because we got to visit all sorts of places that we could not dream of getting to otherwise. The Burton Dassett hills were one particular favourite, I recall. My brother Jim also worked for Jack at one time as a delivery lad cycling round the district with a big heavy push bike that had a basket on the front.

For general groceries we visited the Co-op on Queens Road, the big Art Deco emporium with the Co-op Hall over the top of it. I was sent there on a regular basis with a list of items on a piece of paper my mam had scribbled, and even if my mam sent me down the Co-op today to pick up some stuff I would still be able to recite the divvy number. In those days, the Co-op was not a supermarket where the staff trusted you to fill your own basket: you handed the list in or told them what you wanted and they assembled your groceries and put them in a bag for you. In the cooked meat department, they had a big rotary cutting disc for the ham, which was sliced fresh from a large piece to order. I remember standing there fearfully watching the assistant as he pressed the meat into this horrible spinning blade, expectant any minute for him to slice his fingers off. He never did of course. I wonder what health and safety people would make of it today.

One of Nuneaton's greatest features is its weekly street market. In fact, in this day and age, I believe it is the town's only redeeming feature. Heaven knows what the town centre would be like without it. Back in the 1950s, it was as good as it is today. Nothing has changed. I rather think that the market is, in fact, better now than it was back then, through the sheer variety of stuff you can buy these days. This is where private enterprise has flourished. Saturday was a big day out in our family. The distaff side, my mam and my granny, went in stately procession into town to do their weekly shop. There are two things I particularly remember back then. The first it that potatoes were still covered with soil, so instead of buying a baking potato and putting it straight into the oven, as you do today, it had to be vigorously scrubbed to get the muck off it. The second was my mother judiciously examining apples and repeatedly picking them up and putting them down. A drawn-out process when I could hardly see the difference between them. I dread to thing how many grubby fingerprints were on those apples, but it did us no harm apparently. She also carried out this process of fine selection with all the fruit and vegetables she bought, looking inside the leaves of cabbages and lettuces for grubs, or fruit for wormholes. Modern shoppers at the Co-op, Asda or Sainsbury's have it easy compared to back then. Whether the stuff tasted better I have no idea. One thing seems certain: this was all low air miles produce. It was surely grown in England and I cannot think of anything brought in from abroad.

Our diet was very restricted but we did not suffer by it, and my family livened things up occasionally by buying various types of meat products that do not appear on the menu quite so often today. This was mostly offal – liver, kidneys and tripe all appeared on our dining room table regularly. At first, I was fascinated by tripe. My dad loved it and I recall on one occasion that I was tempted to try some just as a means of experiment, because, to be frank it looked awful. I wondered why my dad golloped it down with such relish. So I asked for a piece and tried it, and I was right – it was truly awful, like a rubbery piece of old dog blanket dripping in milk and laced with onions. Yuk! Anyhow, my dad carried on eating it ostentatiously and on occasion I just had to leave the table as its very appearance. My inability to fathom out what he saw in it unsettled me.

My brother kept rabbits, and they won prizes at the 'Fur and Feather' show, but occasionally one or two also ended up on the plate. I remember eating rabbit once but never seemed to have it again. I think my mother drew the line, having seen these creatures gambolling around the hutch a few days before.

Another feature of town life was that there were no supermarkets as we know them today, but lots and lots of corner shops. I have occasionally wondered how these places made a profit, but I supposed they were often a

Bridge Street was a favourite street of mine because it was so narrow. Old towns were enhanced by these tight thoroughfares. It made the market place more pleasurable as the wide space opened out in front of you. (*Reg. Bull*)

second income. While the old man had a job down the pit, in a brickyard or in the factory, his wife had a little shop, and what small business there was could be offset by being able to source groceries at wholesale prices. Where we lived in Norman Avenue, the corner shop we used most was Mrs Buckler's on the corner of Princes Street. I popped in regularly on my way to school to buy sweets, a comic or an ice cream, and my family might buy a few groceries from there if they had run out of something. When Granny Lee was alive, she could call in on the way back from work in Courtaulds canteen, as it was on her route home. To be fair, it was easier, cheaper and more advantageous to nip down to the Co-op on Queens Road. In my mind's eye, I can still see Mrs Buckler now in her tiny shop with a fairly comprehensive range of tins, vegetables, bread, comics, papers and magazines, a bit like Ronnie Barker in the television comedy programme *Open All Hours*, but on a very modest scale. I don't think Mrs Buckler had a husband when I knew her, so as a widow it must have been a very precarious existence. How long she lived if she survived the '60s I do not know, but by the '70s the shop and adjacent properties had become an electrical contractor's business.

I remember as well that on the odd occasion I would go round for lunch to the house of my two Aunts (Emma and May) in the Kingsway. They were the sisters of my Granddad Percy Carter and, having lost their boyfriends during the First World War, and due to the shortage of men immediately after the War, they never married. They looked after my great-grandmother until she died in 1939. They were not short of a bob or two as the family had been quite wealthy, being builders in Attleborough originally. I am not sure why I went there for lunch other than the fact that my mum, dad and granny were working. As it was the holidays, it was necessary to feed me outside the normal arrangements, but they happily served lunch and I always remember that it was a cooked meal. One day, Auntie Emma served meat and two veg with a great dollop of mustard on the side. She said I would like it, and by crikey it was hot. I reckon that my addiction to mustard and anything as tangy goes back to that single point in my history. There were no curries back then but I love them now, or anything as spicily flavourful.

Another great treat was fish and chips. Our family, without fail, purchased these from Arthur's chip shop in Queens Road, and after my Granny Lee died and we weren't so rigid on the 'fish on Fridays' routine, our Saturday lunchtime arrangements changed to fish and chips. We weren't the only ones, as the queue to be served snaked out of the door and quite a few yards into the street. I did not much care for standing in a queue outside a chip shop in the street. Quite a few packed Midland Red buses passed on the way up Stockingford or into town, and I might be seen by little girls I had a crush on as they looked out of the bus windows. For this reason, I kept my collar up and tried to preserve my anonymity as best I could for the short time I stood outside on the pavement.

# Chapter Nine

# Trainspotting

I must have first taken up trainspotting in the mid-1950s. The reason I can remember this is because my old Granny Lee took me to visit her friend Mrs Bertha Rudkin (who lost her husband in the First World War) who lived in Vernon's Lane and whose house backed onto the railway line to Birmingham. Something about that visit has stuck in my mind to this day. As Granny died in 1957, I estimate this episode must have happened around 1956. The old ladies went about their business, having a good old natter and leaving me with a glass of pop and a plate of biscuits. I can remember looking out of Mrs Rudkin's back window and seeing an endless procession of steam trains trundling by. Then, suddenly and without warning, a green diesel multiple unit zipped by. I was mortified. I knew modernisation was coming but this was the first time I had seen one of these diesel gadgets. I was sad because even back then I saw them as a threat to my beloved steam trains. I was old fashioned and nostalgic before my time. I was eight!

I have always had a peculiar love-hate relationship with my railway hobby. In many ways, I class myself as a railway historian rather than a railway enthusiast, although I have an abiding passion for travelling by train, and the faster, smoother cleaner and more modern the train the better. In recent years, this comes out of necessity, since I work in London a lot and am forced to travel there two or three times a week, so car travel is not an option I chose. There are some people in business I know who can never be divorced from their large company cars. Usually, if I arrange to meet them in London (or elsewhere) for a business appointment, they are always either late, cannot find a parking spot, or if they do are so distracted by the parking meter or time on the limited parking street, and the meeting has to be abandoned while they sort their car out. So yes, I stick to riding the rails, thank you! Back to the '50s.

*Patriot* 4-6-0 No. 45539 heads a down fitted freight through Nuneaton station in the early '50s.

It was scenes like this that excited us. Lovely old steamers like the *Patriot* coming and going. The big gantry above the engine's tender would tilt its tall signals upwards and we knew we were in for a treat. Which snorting express would hove into view? There was so much choice it was mind boggling. You can see how the loco shed hid the approach of the expresses. Our nerves were on edge for whole minutes at a time.

An 8F 2-8-0 brings a freight train through Nuneaton past Ashby Junction on the Up line. (*Mike Mensing*)

A Duchess heads a northbound express through Ashby Junction.

A Royal Scot 4-6-0 No. 46131 on an Up express in the 1950s through Nuneaton station. This was our everyday trainspotting fare when I was a kid.

Trainspotting filled many of the waking hours not occupied by school or generally larking about. There was a routine to it. During school holidays, we ensconced ourselves outside Nuneaton steam sheds, by the scout hut at the bottom of Glebe Road. This was a great position for watching the drama unfold. We had action on the main line, the line to Leicester and the line to Coventry, as well as countless comings and goings on the shed. Long, balmy days of number taking unfolded. During term time, I went down the loco shed at the weekends and sometimes in the evening. Another favoured location was at Ashby Junction, north of the station, where we could observe action on the main line, the Birmingham line and the line to Market Bosworth, with its procession of coal trains. This tended to be more of a summer location as it was a fair trek out of town.

The greatest drama though was when the 'down peg' (signal for northbound trains) for the main line went up and we knew we were in for a real buzz. The steam shed obliterated the view of the down main line so we never knew exactly what was coming, but we could hear it getting closer. Some of my mates could guess from the sound what class of engine was in charge by the noise getting closer and had a fairly accurate hit rate but for me it was just a guess. Then, as

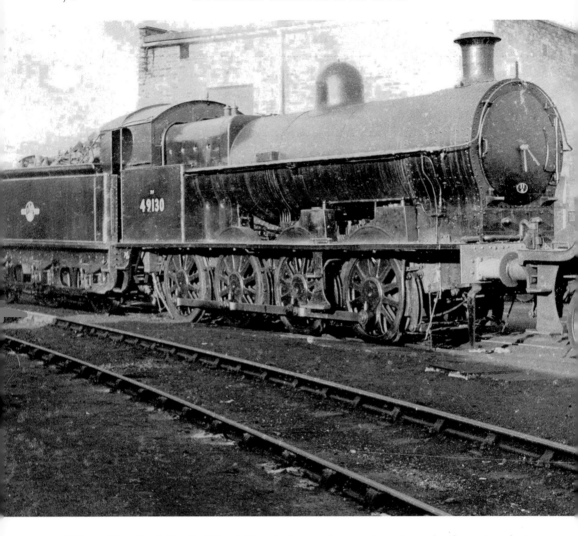

A Super D or Duck 8 – the 'Norah Batty' of steam locomotives. A regular favourite of mine at Nuneaton.

Next to the Coventry line signal gantry on the left can be seen a huddle of kids. Could one of those be me I wonder? This was our regular vantage point with fine views over the south of the station and approaching trains coming in and movements on to the shed yard. The wooden level crossing, just visible, gave us access to the shed on Sundays when it was full of engines. The atmosphere from the green smoke lazily drifting around under the shed roof was pungent. I estimate this picture was taken before 1957.

the sound of the syncopated beat of the exhaust got closer, it would suddenly burst into view and we were in for a treat.

Back in the '50s it was magical because the sheer variety of steam power was a thrill. Any one of these express trains could produce a *Duchess*, or a *Princess*, a Royal Scot or a Jubilee, a Patriot, a Black Five, a Britannia, and on the odd occasion other Standard Classes such as a Clan or a Standard 5. Any of these snorting monsters could burst into view and for us, at least, it was the luck of the draw. You really needed your notebooks in order to record the variety of motive power on view. Nowadays, efficient though the electrics diesels are, they are so boring. We were never bored. These things were real, living, breathing, steamy, fiery beasts – high drama on wheels.

I often wonder what it used to be like, before I was born, when the old London North Western types held sway. The thrill of the approach of a Jumbo, a Precursor, a Prince of Wales, an Experiment, a Lady of the Lake or a Claughton – I wonder what that must have been like. I remember reading somewhere that the puny little Jumbos were thrashed so unmercifully to keep time by their crews that the entire contents of the firebox were blown out of the chimney and rained down as burning cinders on the engine's cab roof, but the fireman had to keep shovelling to feed the insatiable appetite of his engine for coal, which produced this pyrotechnic display.

A sight I regrettably missed, although it had not happened much before my early trainspotting years, was to see a 2P 4-4-0 paired with a Duchess on an express. Old railway mates have told me about this practice, which some official had decided needed to be done because if a Duchess had fifteen coaches, a pilot engine was required to provide enough vacuum to the coach brakes. The little 2P was chosen as a pilot engine because its driving wheels at 6 feet 9 inches were the same as the Pacific's, so it was figured that it could keep up with its massive companion. Many a footplate man, when charged with this job, was very upset. The Duchess did not need an impediment to its progress – a puny 2P stuck to its front buffer beam, and the hapless 2P crew knew it. It was made especially worse if the 2P was the old Midland variety with a low tender body. The 2P crew could see at their back the frightful snorting maw of a smoke box of the great engine behind, which threatened to kick them out of the way so it could get on, or climb all over them in a big pile up. The whole thing came to a head one day, when a 2P crew were so traumatised by the job that they got off their engine at Stafford and said 'we ain't going any further'. The Union stepped in and the practice was stopped, but what a show for the trainspotter.

Our trainspotting routine in the summer holidays was marked by going to the little grocer's shop on the corner of Wheat Street and King Edward Road and buying a frozen Jubbly. This was a very large triangular block of frozen orange juice that lasted for miles, or quite a good part of the morning at any rate. As we sucked it through the cardboard wrapper and picked it up and put it down, we fumbled for our notebooks as yet another then another express burst through, or a local rattled down the Coventry or Leicester line. The only down side was that by the time we had finished our lips had turned orange. My Mam knew when we had been sucking on a Jubbly because when I got home she would attack my face with the flannel.

We knew what time to go home for our tea of course because we could hear Courtaulds clock chime. It was heard all over town, and another crop of train numbers were underlined in our combined volumes. I still treasure all of my early trainspotting books.

A Black Five 4-6-0 heads a northbound express train through Trent Valley station.

The shed yard.

Bursting through Nuneaton station. A *Britannia* on an Up Manchester Express.

Most of my pals had their preferences back in our trainspotting days. Usually Duchesses (Semis we called them) or Princesses (Princes), or Royal Scots (Scots) or Jubilees (Jubes). Everyone liked, without exception, the Patriots (Pates), but my eye was drawn to a rather unusual love object, which maybe tells me something about my character. I went for the old 'Duck Eight', seen in the previous image at a moment of relaxation on Nuneaton shed. I do not know why. They were Nuneaton's common and ubiquitous freight engines up until 1962, but they just had bags of charm. What really appealed to me was their performance with a heavy freight under labouring conditions. These old engines really came alive. The smoke, the steam, the noise; it was all so deliciously exquisite. No engine I have ever seen before or since had it all in one package. Over the years, I have been privileged to know and associate with several old drivers and firemen at Nuneaton shed. They have told me tales of the old 'Duck Eight', or 'Super D' in railwayman's parlance, which is now the term I use. I was enthralled by it.

The old timers I knew in later years, as well as myself, were great fans of *Last of the Summer Wine*. Knowing the characters in that comedy series, we likened the old 'Super D' to the Norah Batty of steam locos. It shared all the same characteristics with that formidable lady. The heavy cast-iron wheels for a start reminded us of Norah's wrinkly stockings. The austere design was Norah too. And the men who came into contact with her suffered the same harsh treatment. When it came to the subject of housekeeping, i.e. getting a train from A to B in an efficient manner, there was nothing finer than the 'Super D'.

One old-timer said a long departed pal of ours, an old fireman, would kick the wall and mutter unmentionable words when he found he had a 'D' for the day after reporting for duty at Nuneaton shed and checking the roster. It was that sort of relationship. But the old timer who related this story told me that having a 'Super D' for the day did not faze him, because he knew he would get the job done in an unfussy manner. Whether it was a freight to Bletchley, Stafford or Willesden, the old 'D' would get him there, albeit slowly. He said 'give me an old "D" any day', and we nicknamed him 'Compo' after making those comments.

One thing I remember about the 'D', though, was one iconic day sitting in Manor Park School in a classroom overlooking the Abbey Street station to Birmingham railway line. I noticed what can only be described as an apparition heaving into view. This object was completely wrapped in white steam and, as it slowed for a signal, I could not tell what class of engine it was, so dense was the shroud of steam. Then the signal bounced upwards, and this thing started to move slowly forward. As it did, the smoke box door nosed through the steam. It was a 'D'! A magnificent performance was about to unfold. The two old cylinder 'D's had a distinctive sound, two deep blasts followed by two lighter blasts, something like 'CHUFF CHUFF, chuff chuff', and so on. Well, as this old bird collared her heavy load, the noise was distinctive. Its syncopated beat got louder and louder. There was a throaty aspect to it as well. The old 'D' had developed a characteristic asthmatic wheeze, like an old cigarette smoker on sixty a day. To top it all was the incessant hiss of steam from one or more of its orifices. This, mixed in with the elaborate chuffing, was a wonderful sound as this old gal set to work, gathered speed and cemented for me a lifelong appreciation of the products of Crewe works before 1923.

# Chapter Ten

# Entertainment

Throughout my life, I have understood that boys are wired differently to girls. I cannot remember the number of times I have talked about my passion for the Goons to be met with pitying stares from the females in my orbit. 'Are you mad?', well yes, probably. And it all started in the '50s. As I mentioned before, fun and excitement were very thin on the ground back then. Some of our meagre scraps of these precious commodities came from the cinema and the radio or, more likely, the Saturday matinee when I think of being down the Ritz with my mates. We were nicely turned out because, after all, the little girls went too, and unlike school (where you could be humiliated any time by the teacher), we could act 'cool' at the Ritz. Most of the girls were from other schools, so they did not know if you had been picked on by the teacher in front of your classmates. It did not work for me much, though, I only got to sit next to a girl once and put my arms around her. You could only get away with this in the dark as your mates were hard pressed to see what you were up to, and of course there was no kissing and cuddling – this was the '50s and I was barely eleven. As soon as the lights turned up, I resumed a demeanour of sitting there arms crossed and strictly 'without prejudice', as though I was just in this seat, you understand, under duress. Anyway, I got away with it but me and the girl never did sit next to each other again. The stress and effort was too much, and at any rate it distracted me from the film (I comforted myself with this at any rate). The following week she was sitting next to another boy with his arms round her I noticed.

The Ritz Saturday matinee served up a fairly innocuous diet of B movies, the sort you wouldn't watch today on daytime television even if there was nothing else on and you were stuck at home with a plaster on your leg. They were generally – in a word – terrible. 'Cowboys and Indians' were a major part of the diet. I could never understand how smartly turned out some of these cowboys

The Ritz.

were too. Roy Rogers and the Lone Ranger, for example, looked as though they had just stepped out of the shower and were attending a fancy dress ball dragged up in cowboy uniform. Where was their five o'clock shadow? Their three-day stubble or their beards and the sweat and dust, blood and saliva, or runny noses? Even after racing across the Midwest on their galloping horses their hats stayed on, their faces looked as fresh as though my mother had had a go at them with her ubiquitous flannel. It was so unbelievable. Even the sci-fi movies had miserable plywood sets and unconvincing extraterrestrials. Green martians were favoured, but my image of them at the flicks and in the Dan Dare comic strip are mixed up today. So much for sci-fi movies! In fact, in all the films we saw back then, I cannot remember one, although I can remember Picken's Batch Bar. I can still taste those batches even today.

Sunday, however, was the highlight of the week, because everylunchtime we turned on the radio and my brother and I were away with the fairies! Well, Eccles, Bluebottle, Little Jim, Neddy Seagoon, Major Bloodnock, Henry Crun and Minnie Bannister. You name it, we were there. If you look back to those dreary days of the '50s, the Goons shone out like a beacon. They were new, outrageous, fresh and the great thing about radio then was you could imagine these mad characters in your own mind's eye as you wanted them to appear on the television set in your head. It made them more believable. It concentrated the madness, stirred up the cobwebs in your brain, and made you feel a bit special too. Because you got it, and a lot of people didn't. I still feel that way and pity people when discussing this they say 'don't know what you see in the Goons!' What a shame for them!

Abbey Street and the corner
of Stratford Street. (*Reg. Bull*)

A view of Newdigate Street where it joins Newdigate Square.

Bridge Street in the 1950s.

*Inset:* Abbey Street and the Ritz corner, opposite the High Street.

When Powell's shop was demolished it exposed a row of old court cottages, which had been used for many years as stores for paint, wallpaper and decorator's accessories.

Remember this row of shops in Queens Road? (*Reg. Bull, Ruby Atkins Collection*)

At one time a statue of a mother and two children stood in front of the museum in Riversley Park. Later the statue was removed. This photograph was taken of it on 11 May 1958. (*Geoff Edmands*)

A row of very interesting terraced houses once stood at the top of Wheat Street just before you got to the underpass to the Trent Valley railway and then on into Oaston Road. (*Geoff Edmands*)

# Chapter Eleven

# An Afterthought
# The Magic of Skegness

I remember back in the '80s, when I was working for an engineering company in Stratford-upon-Avon, and my mam and dad were still alive, they had yet another week's holiday in Skegness. They travelled by bus, and I said I would catch up with them when they returned the following week. On the Monday or Tuesday, my boss asked me to go over to Sleaford or Spalding, as a firm over there needed to see us about a job that needed to be done. So I trundled off, called on the firm for the meeting, which did not take as long as expected, and around lunchtime found myself pitched out into the Lincolnshire countryside in the knowledge I wasn't expected back at the factory that day. I thought to myself, I am quite close to Skeggy I wonder if I could find my parents, surprise them and treat them to a cup of tea. Bear in mind that mobile phones had not been invented back then, so trying to liaise with them that way was impossible. I had to go on instincts and, knowing the time of day, figure out where in the town they might be. So I pulled up in Skeggy, parked the car, and going on pure judgement made my way to the Sun Castle. And there they were, sitting outside the Sun Castle on a warm summer's day enjoying a nice cup of tea. I can always remember the scene now, as I trudged down the path towards them my mam looked up at me and a wonderful range of expressions passed over her face. She looked up as I approached from a distance and her face passed from mild interest into who this approaching stranger was, through disbelief into surprise. She said to my dad, who hadn't looked up by that time, 'Ay up, here's our Peter!' Both asked how I could possibly have found them, but somehow I knew where they would be. That was what Skeggy meant to us. It was ingrained in our psyche.

Because my brother Jim was ten years older than me, we did not knock around together much back then. In the 1950s, he had discovered girls and motorbikes and I was still hurtling about on wooden trollies and being suspicious of the opposite sex. Talking to him now, though, it seems when he was my age he did much the same sort of thing, playing over the Cloddies with his mates in the street, and breeding rabbits, which he did with some success I am told (later on it was budgies). He told me a couple of stories he remembered that had taken place shortly after the Second World War ended. The local council had supplied galvanised dustbins, which were chained to the trees in the street. It was a time of rationing and these bins were to collect vegetable waste, potato peelings and lettuce and cabbage leaves to be used as pig food. It was collected every week and carted off to be processed. Imagine having stinking dustbins cluttering up the streets, which might have collected any sort of garbage for all we know. This practice evidently lasted into the '50s until the complaints about the smell put paid to the practice. Anyway, every so often, the council came round and emptied them. Come October and November, when fireworks became readily available in the shops, our Jim, following the emptying of the bins, would randomly go round shoving fizzing bangers in them, then retiring to a distance. The boom was so resonant inside the empty bin it blew the lids off. I guess it was better than just lighting the banger, retreating to a safe distance and waiting for the bang. It added a frisson of fun watching the lid being displaced. Heaven knows what the burnt residue explosive powder did to the contents of the bin and the digestive system of the pigs.

Another aspect that we forget about many of our domestic streets was that when built the council planted neat rows of trees, Norman Avenue, as its name implied, was an avenue of trees, and the trees in the street were a nice feature. After a while these matured, and had a lovely abundant crop of foliage on them. Every now and again, the council came round and cruelly cropped them so that they were almost denuded of leaves and branches.

'Auntie Kate' was a surrogate member of the family, and her daughter Carol was like a sister to us. Kate and Carol were jolly and great fun and I always associate them with light heartedness and silly banter. However, one day our Jim took this good humoured nature to an extreme and came unstuck, literally. Auntie Kate lived just down the road and had one of these large avenue trees outside her front room window across a narrow front garden. One night, our Jim, determined to have a bit of fun with Auntie Kate, got a thumb tack, a bobbin of black thread from our Mam's sewing case and a metal nut. He crept up and quietly stuck the thumb tack into the woodwork above Auntie Kate's window (the curtains were drawn, but the light was on), wound the cotton round it, threaded the cotton through the nut and retired to climb the tree and hide in the foliage a few yards away with the other end of the cotton. Remember it was a dark night, and the cotton was invisible. He then proceeded to slacken the cotton so that the nut was thrust against the window. There must have been a bit of planning gone into this daft exercise. Auntie Kate and Carol were in the front room so the light was on. The nut went 'clink, clink' on the window, which is not the sort of noise you usually hear, so the front door was opened, Jim pulled the cotton tight and the nut disappeared into the night. Auntie Kate came out, looked around, saw no one and returned inside. It happened again, the same routine and out she came, looking around and examining the window. She saw nothing and returned indoors. This must have happened four or five times at random intervals, by which time Auntie Kate was very perplexed indeed, until she looked up and saw something unusual above the window – what appeared to be a metal object suspended in mid-air. On closer inspection she could just make out the faint sign of the cotton and its trace heading towards the abundant foliage on the tree. She returned indoors, the nut clinked on the window again and on this occasion Auntie Kate came out from the back gate armed with a wooden clothes prop and poked our Jim out of the tree. A few words were said and I understand the incident was not repeated. Our Jim got on with other boyish pranks.

*Above:* Queens Road in the 1950s.

*Right:* Tatler was a cinema at one time, but was a grocer's when I knew it.

Newdigate Square.

Where the current annexe to the town hall stands in Coton Road there was a stretch of garden with a water fountain which amused the townspeople for over fifty years before it was taken away for the new council offices. (*Geoff Edmands*)

Nuneaton post office. (*Geoff Edmands*)

This bridge conveyed the Nuneaton–Coventry railway line over the Attleborough Road.

*Inset*: Weddington Road railway bridge.

The Wharf Inn, in the centre of the postcard above, was built by the Newdigate estate. It was to be a significant place on the canal system in its day, with sleeping quarters for boatmen as well as a warehouse and boat repair facilities.

Coventry Canal.

For several generations the Wem Brook in the Pingle Fields was adapted as a paddling pool for children. There were carefully constructed concrete steps into it and the brook was cleaned out at this point so kids could safely paddle.

# Conclusion

When I started to write these memories down, I thought it would be good to leave some recollections of my life as a child for my own family. First, I serialised this in the *Nuneaton News* in the hope that others might come forward from that era and make contact again. No one did, of course, such is the power of publicity! Nevertheless, it has been a worthwhile exercise because, for one thing, as I set out to put fingers to keyboard I only had a few clear memories of yesteryear. The physical process of writing them down helped me to transport myself back to those formative times. Gradually, a veil lifted from so many hidden aspects of the life I had entirely forgotten. It was an enlightening experience. I was also keen to work out why I had gone down the particular path of life I took and how my childhood experiences shaped my future years. On the surface, my later years have had little to do with my early upbringing. I got married and went into construction engineering. My school years had nothing do with that, other than making me competent in the three Rs. My parental influences have always been important, though. My mother was a very proud and hard-working person. My dad was a role model for us all, an ardent Socialist of the old school. He would have had little time for politics today. Things were black and white to my dad, and the idea of socialism being reborn as New Labour would have disturbed him. Whereas today, I distrust the political class, realising that the clear division between the working, middle and ruling classes no longer matters. What does matter is common sense. My dad worked hard at his job and carried his ideas of public service into voluntary trade union activities way beyond retirement. Immaculate cleanliness and good dress sense were important principles to my mother, born out of necessity. It took a lot of work to keep everything in her household clean and I followed her example. Others, unfortunately, are less inclined towards the benefits of personal presentation. Our family were kind and considerate to everybody they knew. We did not know anyone in those days who thought it was smart to be devious. People like that might have been around but we never met them. Our entire family and their friends were as straightforward as could be. We never had harsh words or fell out with anyone. There was nothing in our experience to have harsh words about. And the strange thing is I never remember a row, other than a few corrections from our parents if we stepped out of line. Words were enough. We knew if we had passed over the line that should never be crossed.

# Acknowledgements

Colin Yorke, Jim Lee, Vic Holloway, Alan Cook, John Jeavons, Geoff Edmands, Reg. Bull, Ruby Atkins and Madge Edmands.

## Nuneaton Through Time
Peter Lee

This fascinating selection of photographs traces some of the many ways in which Nuneaton has changed and developed over the last century.

978 1 84868 595 6
96 pages, full colour

Available from all good bookshops or order direct from our website www.amberleybooks.com

# ALSO AVAILABLE FROM AMBERLEY PUBLISHING

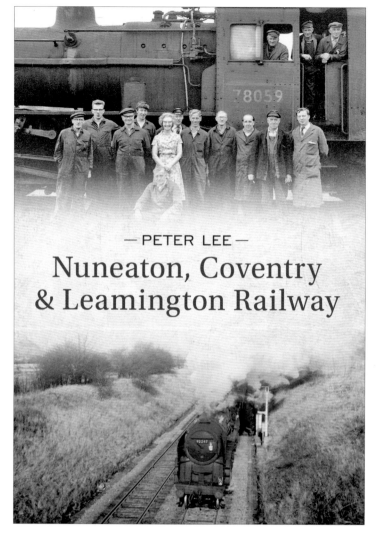

## Nuneaton, Coventry & Leamington Railway
### Peter Lee

*Nuneaton, Coventry & Leamington Railway* documents how the railways linking these two important Warwickshire towns were faithfully served by steam locomotion for many years.

978 1 4456 0661 3
160 pages

Available from all good bookshops or order direct
from our website www.amberleybooks.com